SUPER MEN OF THE BIBLE

by Julie Lavender

Carson-Dellosa Christian Publishing • Greensboro, North Carolina

TABLE OF CONTENTS

SUPER MEN OF THE BIBLE

INTRODUCTION

Kids are naturally drawn to comics—especially if there are heroes involved! *Super Men of the Bible* will have children learning, laughing, and growing in their faith as they explore the hero-hearts and life lessons of 15 of the most powerful heroes of the Bible.

Each interactive lesson in *Super Men of the Bible* is designed to be used several ways, depending on the students, classroom setting, and specific needs of the teacher.

Super Man Lesson: Teachers can use this page as a guide to create a custom class lesson, or, to duplicate for each student to follow along or work on individually. To help the students connect with the story, there are places on the page to record their responses.

The speech bubble warm-up question, asked by the hero himself, gets the students thinking about what they will learn. Then, after hearing the Bible story, the "Power Up!" section will power up the students' hearts with challenges that they can apply in their own lives.

My Story: On this page, the students get to be heroes in their own stories! This page may be duplicated for each student so that he can reflect and respond to the question on the page by creating his own comic strip. Each character-building lesson is reinforced through an "Action!" activity that can be completed as a class or individually at home.

Make the students' comic strips come alive with various speech balloons. Copy the speech balloon template (page 64) for each student. Allow students to cut out and glue the speech balloons to their comic strips. An extra comic strip panel template is also included on page 64.

Skit–Toons and Power Tunes: The life-lessons of these super men of the Bible will spring to life through these child-friendly skits and songs. Duplicate the pages for the class so that everyone can participate or use the page as a guide to create your own custom skit!

Puzzle Page: Encourage the students to use their super brain power to complete the fun puzzle page at the conclusion of each lesson.

Create Your Own Comic Book! Students can create their own comic book as a way to reflect, respond, and remember the lessons in a personal way. Here's how:

- At the beginning of the unit, encourage students to design their own comic book cover. Use blank sheets of paper or colorful construction paper.

- Use three-pronged pocket folders, or simply fasten the pages with yarn, ribbon, or brad fasteners.

- Include the Super Man Lesson, My Story, and Skit-Toon pages in the comic books, if desired, as reminders of the lesson.

OBEDIENT NOAH

Noah was a good man who loved God. One day, God told Noah that he was going to destroy the earth with a flood because of everyone's disobedience on earth. God also told Noah to build a huge boat, called an ark, so that he, his family, and a male and female of every animal could be saved.

Noah obeyed God, even though there were probably people who thought he was crazy for building such a large boat! When Noah finished the ark, he gathered the animals and all of his family, and went on the boat—just as God told him to do.

Then, the rains came. For 40 days and nights, it rained and rained. Every living thing on land was destroyed.

When the water dried up, Noah, his family, and all of the animals on the ark were safe because of Noah's obedience to God. As a sign of His love and His promise to never destroy the earth by flood again, God created a beautiful rainbow in the sky.

"WE MUST OBEY GOD RATHER THAN MEN!" ACTS 5:29

EVER NOT FOLLOW INSTRUCTIONS AND END UP WITH A MESS?

Write about or draw a picture of a time you forgot to follow instructions.

POWER UP!

Obedience is the one word that best describes the life of Noah. When everyone on Earth turned away from God, Noah remained obedient to God's commands. When God gave Noah exact instructions on how to build an ark, Noah obeyed every Word—down to the last detail. What would have happened to the ark had Noah not obeyed God's plan? It would have sunk! Because of his obedience, Noah and his family were saved. Do you obey God in all circumstances—down to the last detail?

✦ On the back of this paper, draw or write something that illustrates the question below:

Is there one of God's instructions that is very hard for you to obey? Write a prayer asking for God's help.

OBEDIENT NOAH

Now, it's your turn to be the hero of the story. Write or draw your own comic strip!

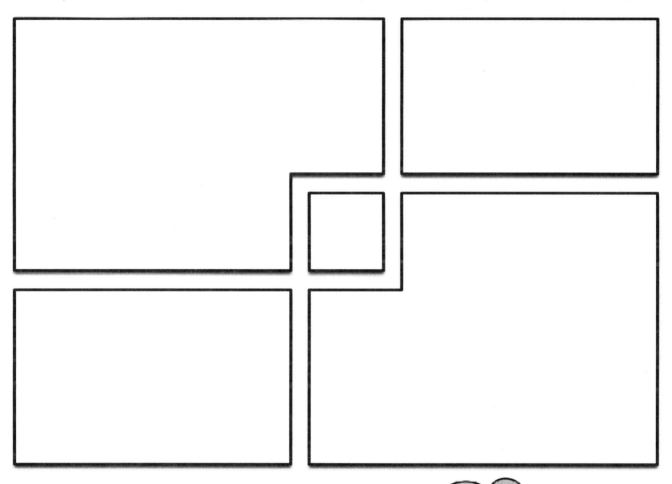

"WE MUST OBEY GOD RATHER THAN MEN!" ACTS 5:29

OUR GOD REIGNS

WITH NOTHING ELSE TO DO BUT WAIT OUT THE RAIN, NOAH WRITES THE FIRST HYMN.

ACTION! Cut a white paper plate in half. Color a rainbow on the plate. On the rainbow, write, "I will obey God by . . ." Cut out four large raindrops from white or blue paper. On each raindrop, write the ways you will obey God. Cut four pieces of yarn and tape one end to the back of the raindrops and the other end to the back of the rainbow. Hang it in a place where you will see it everyday to be reminded to obey God's commands—just like Noah!

OBEDIENT NOAH

God commands us to obey—even if it is not popular!

Cast: *Two girls to play Sara and Anna*

Sara: Anna, let's stop by that new store on the way home from school today. I heard they have ice cream cones!

Anna: That sounds good, but I don't think I can.

Sara: Why?

Anna: I told my dad I would come right home from school. I have to watch my little brother.

Sara: Baby-sitting again? Boy, you sure have a boring life. Come on, your dad won't know, it will only take a minute. I'll even buy you an ice cream cone!

Anna: Well . . .

Sara: Well . . . what? Look, you could always say Miss Smith kept you after school to talk about the school play if your dad asks why you're late.

Anna: I don't want to lie. Plus, my dad told me to come right home today.

Sara: I don't understand why you always have to do everything your parents say all of the time. It's boring!

Anna: I'm trying to do what God commands us to do, which is to obey our parents. When we obey our parents, we're obeying God. Besides, it's not boring when my parents trust me and I know I'm doing what's right.

Sara: Well, I haven't been obedient lately. My mom told me to clean my room yesterday, and I still haven't done it. And I know she won't be happy when she finds out. I think I better go straight home, too, and get cleaning!

POWER TUNES (SING TO THE TUNE OF "I'M A LITTLE TEAPOT")

Have fun acting out this Power Tune that tells the story of Noah.

God told Noah, "Listen.	*Hand to ear.*
Here's my plan.	*Open both hands like a book.*
You build a big ark.	*Motion as if hammering.*
I'll lend a hand.	*Extend one hand in front—as an offering to help.*
Gather up the animals	*Wave one hand as if saying, "Come here."*
Two by two.	*Hold up 2 fingers.*
Then climb aboard	*Walk in place.*
And I'll save you."	*Make fists with both hands, wrists together, then pull apart (as if being set free).*

OBEDIENT NOAH

God commanded Noah to gather animals two by two. Help him find the animal on the right that matches the pictures on the left by coloring the matching animal pictures.

7

FAITHFUL ABRAHAM

God told Abraham to pack up and leave his country, his people, and his home. Boy, was he surprised! God did not tell him where he was going, or why he wanted him to travel hundreds of miles away. Yet, Abraham obeyed God's call.

Abraham put his faith in God. He knew that if God asked him to go, God would take care of him.

God called Abraham to a new land and promised to make him into a great nation. God also said He would bless Abraham and his family. God even changed his name from Abram to Abraham—meaning "father of many." Abraham did not ask God "how or why"? He placed all of his faith in God.

Abraham's faith was strong. Even as he traveled far from the land that he knew to a strange new place, he remained faithful to God and God was faithful to Abraham.

HAVE YOU EVER TRAVELED TO A NEW AND STRANGE PLACE?

NOW FAITH IS BEING SURE OF WHAT WE HOPE FOR AND CERTAIN OF WHAT WE DO NOT SEE. HEBREWS 11:1

Write about or draw a picture of a new place you have visited recently.

Power Up!

Why did Abraham obey God? Abraham placed faith in God when he obeyed and left his friends and home to travel to a new land. God promised to build a great nation through Abraham—and Abraham had faith in this promise!

God may lead us in a new direction to do even greater things for Him. It may not make sense to us, but that is where faith comes in. Do not let the comfort of where you are now keep you from faithfully following God's direction—wherever it may lead!

✦ On the back of this paper, draw something that illustrates the question below:

What direction is God leading you?

FAITHFUL ABRAHAM

Now, it's your turn to be the hero of the story. Write or draw your own comic strip!

NOW FAITH IS BEING SURE OF WHAT WE HOPE FOR AND CERTAIN OF WHAT WE DO NOT SEE. HEBREWS 11:1

I TOLD YOU HE SAID CANAAN, NOT CARIBBEAN.

 **ACTION!**

For the next week, do a little stargazing with your family. Think about how God is like the stars and the moon—sometimes He is easy to see, and sometimes, He isn't easy to see. But no matter what, God is always there. Even when we cannot see the moon or the stars at night, we know that they are still in the sky. Faith is being certain of what we *do not* see.

FAITHFUL ABRAHAM

SKIT-TOON

Act out this skit in a modified version of Follow the Leader. The first time through, the teacher should play the part of God and let the students play the part of Abraham and say the lines in chorus. At the end, lead the class in a follow-the-leader style walk around the classroom. After showing the class what to do, choose a child to play the part of God and let the rest of the students say Abraham's words.

Cast: *God (leader), Abraham (entire class)*

God: Abraham, Abraham, leave your home and go.

Abraham: Where am I going? How will I know?

God: Abraham, Abraham, listen and obey.

Abraham: I trust in Your words, I will do as You say.

God: Abraham, Abraham, have faith in me.

Abraham: I'll have faith in you. Watch me and you'll see.

POWER TUNES (SING TO THE TUNE OF "DID YOU EVER SEE A LASSIE?")

Before singing, form a circle with one child in the middle. As the group begins to sing, "Walk this way and that way . . .," have the person in the middle do some sort of movement. The other students mimic that student's movement for the rest of the song. Continue with other students suggesting movements as you sing.

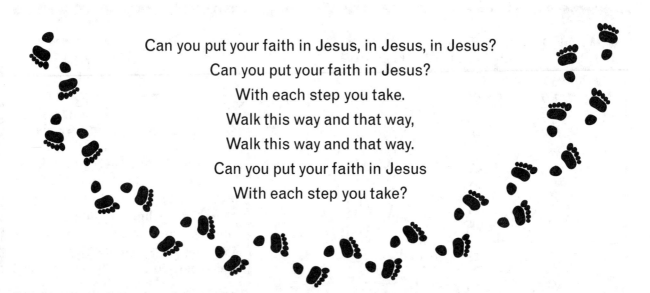

Can you put your faith in Jesus, in Jesus, in Jesus?
Can you put your faith in Jesus?
With each step you take.
Walk this way and that way,
Walk this way and that way.
Can you put your faith in Jesus
With each step you take?

ABRAHAM'S MAZE

Help Abraham and Sarah find their way to their new home in Canaan. Along the way, find the item listed below that they will need to take on the trip.

HIDDEN PICTURES

tunic	sandals	loaf of bread	oil jar	donkey	tent

PEACEMAKER ISAAC

Isaac, the son of Abraham, believed in God. God blessed Isaac with much wealth in crops, herds of animals, and servants.

The Philistines, who lived around Isaac, became jealous of his wealth. They filled his water wells with earth so that Isaac's animals would not have water. Then, they asked him to move away. Although this was unfair, Isaac chose to move away for the sake of peace.

Isaac found and dug new wells two more times. Both times there were disputes on who the wells belonged to. Isaac peacefully gave up the wells and moved on both times. Finally, Isaac found a well that no one else claimed. He thanked God for providing the well and enough land for everyone to live.

Isaac's enemies noticed how peacefully he handled the disputes over the wells. Rather than start a big fight, Isaac had chosen to compromise and be a peacemaker. His enemies respected this and decided to become friends with Isaac. God continued to bless Isaac just as He blessed his father.

MAKE EVERY EFFORT TO LIVE IN PEACE WITH ALL MEN AND TO BE HOLY; WITHOUT HOLINESS NO ONE WILL SEE THE LORD. HEBREWS 12:14

> WHAT HAVE YOU DONE LATELY TO LIVE IN PEACE?

Write about or draw a picture of what *peace* means to you.

POWER UP!

Why were the Philistines jealous of Isaac? What did the Philistines do?

Isaac lived near a desert where water was precious and owning a well was critical to surviving. Plugging up someone's well was a very serious crime back then. Isaac had every right to fight back. Yet, he chose peace. In the end, the Philistines, who had plugged Isaac's wells, respected him for leaving and more importantly, God blessed Isaac for it. What would you give up in order to keep peace?

✦ On the back of this paper, draw something that illustrates the question below:

What effort will you make to live in peace with everyone?

PEACEMAKER ISAAC

Now, it's your turn to be the hero of the story. Write or draw your own comic strip!

ACTION!

Make a "Peace Well" as a reminder to make every effort to live in peace. Horizontally cut a brown paper lunch bag in half. Decorate the bottom half with a stone pattern to create a well. Write *My Peace Well* on the front of the bag. Fold the top of the bag over about one inch. Every time you choose peace this week—like not arguing with others—drop a penny in the well. See how many pennies you have in one week!

MAKE EVERY EFFORT TO LIVE IN PEACE WITH ALL MEN AND TO BE HOLY; WITHOUT HOLINESS NO ONE WILL SEE THE LORD.
HEBREWS 12:14

ISAAC SPREADS PEACE ALL OVER THE LAND.

PEACEMAKER ISAAC

SKIT-TOON

Does Isaac say, "No fair!" when told to look for another well? Act out this Skit-Toon and find out!

Cast: *Isaac and servants, Herdsman 1, 2, and 3.*

Isaac: I have to leave this land and look for another well so I can have water. Come with me. *(Motions to servants. All walk to another area in room, then pretend to dig a well.)*

Herdsman 1: Hey, that's *our* water! You have to find another place for a well!

Isaac: I will go in peace and find another well. *(Isaac and servants walk to another area in room, pretend to dig a well.)*

Herdsman 2: Hey, that's *our* water! You have to find another place for a well!

Isaac: I will go in peace and find another well. *(Isaac and servants walk to another area in room, pretend to dig a well.)*

Herdsman 3: Hey, that's *our* water! You have to find another place for a well!

Isaac: I will go in peace and find another well. *(Isaac and servants walk to another area in room, pretend to dig a well. Stop and look around, and then say)* Finally! This is *our* water! Thank You, God, for giving enough land for everyone!

POWER TUNES (SING TO THE TUNE "THIS LITTLE LIGHT OF MINE")

To act out the song, pretend to dig each time you sing the line, "I'm gonna dig a well," and fold hands in prayer for the last line. Name new animals to replace "sheep" and sing the first verse through several times. Sing the second verse and make a peace sign when you sing, "peace," and point to yourself when singing, "that's what I will do."

Verse 1
I'm gonna dig a well,
So my sheep can drink.
I'm gonna dig a well,
So my sheep can drink.
I'm gonna dig a well,
So my sheep can drink.
Thank You, Lord,
Thank You, Lord, for my well.

Verse 2
I'm gonna live in peace,
That's what I will do.
I'm gonna live in peace,
That's what I will do.
I'm gonna live in peace,
That's what I will do.
Live in peace, every day
Live In peace.

PEACEMAKER ISAAC

STONE WELL CODE PUZZLE

Fill in the missing letters in the clues below to read the message from Isaac.

God blessed _____saac with much wealth.

Isaac's father's _____ame is Abraham.

The _____hilistines asked Isaac to move away.

The people told Isaac that the w_____lls belonged to them.

Isaac chose pea_____e.

DEPENDABLE JACOB

Jacob was living with his uncle, Laban. He did chores in exchange for being able to live with him. Jacob was such a dependable worker, Laban offered to pay him for his work. But, Jacob did not want money. Instead, he wanted to marry Laban's youngest daughter, Rachel. Jacob offered to work for seven years in exchange for Rachel's hand in marriage.

HAVE YOU EVER TRIED TO GET OUT OF DOING YOUR CHORES?

Jacob did just what he had promised. He worked hard for seven years—never going back on his end of the bargain. However, when the seven years were up, Laban tricked Jacob into marrying his oldest daughter, Leah, instead of Rachel.

Jacob was not happy that he had been tricked. Laban told him that he could marry Rachel, too, if he worked another seven years. Jacob agreed and once again, worked dependably for another seven years.

Jacob kept his end of the bargain. Laban knew he could trust Jacob to keep his word because Jacob proved he was dependable.

DON'T OBEY THEM ONLY TO PLEASE THEM WHEN THEY ARE WATCHING. . . . BE SURE YOUR HEART DOES WHAT GOD WANTS. . . . WORK AS IF YOU WERE NOT SERVING PEOPLE BUT THE LORD. EPHESIANS 6:6-7 (NIRV)

Write about or draw a picture of yourself doing a daily chore.

Power Up!

Who was dependable in this story? Jacob built a reputation for being dependable by following through on his chores in exchange for room and board with Laban. Jacob remained reliable and trustworthy while working for Laban for 14 years.

Doing what you say and following through on tasks lets others know you are dependable. Do you complete your chores without being asked?

✦ On the back of this paper, draw something that illustrates the question below:

How can I be more dependable at home? At school?

DEPENDABLE JACOB

Now, it's your turn to be the hero of the story. Write or draw your own comic strip!

ACTION! On a poster board, make a list of all of your chores. On an index card, write *Done* on one side and *Not Done* on the other side. Tape a piece of yarn to the index card, and tape the other end of the yarn to the bottom of your chore poster. Turn the index card to *Not Done* as a reminder to complete all of your chores. Flip the sign to *Done* when all of your chores are finished.

DON'T OBEY THEM ONLY TO PLEASE THEM WHEN THEY ARE WATCHING. . . . EPHESIANS 6:6 (NIRV)

YES, MOM, I'VE DONE ALL MY CHORES! I'VE BEEN WORKING HARD ALL DAY!

Dependable Jacob

Cast: *Two boys to play John and Eric*

John: Hey Eric, let's go! Everyone is waiting for us to play ball.

Eric: Go on ahead without me. I still have some chores left to finish.

John: Go ask your mom if you can do them later. Everyone is waiting!

Eric: Can't.

John: Can't?

Eric: Nope, I can't ask my mom if I can do my chores later.

John: Why not?

Eric: Because she isn't here. Neither is my dad. They went to visit someone and won't be back for a couple of hours.

John: Come on, then! You can finish your chores before they get back and *after* you pitch the perfect game!

Eric: Can't.

John: Can't?

Eric: Nope. They are depending on me to finish all of my chores *now*.

John: But you will finish them—just *after* the game.

Eric: I told my mom and dad I would finish my chores before I'd go out and play. They are depending on me to keep my word.

John: Well, we're depending on you as well. You're our best pitcher!

Eric: You can depend on me *after* I do my chores.

John: Okay, okay. How much do you have to do?

Eric: Sweep out the garage, water the garden, and take out the garbage.

John: I'll water the garden, you sweep out the garage.

Eric: Thanks John! I'm glad I can depend on you to help!

POWER TUNES (SING TO THE TUNE OF "TEN LITTLE INDIANS")

One year, two years, three years working.
Four years, five years, six years working.
Seven years, seven years, seven years working.
Seven years working for Leah.

One year, two years, three years working.
Four years, five years, six years working.
Seven years, seven years, seven years working.
Seven years working for Rachel.

DEPENDABLE JACOB

WORD SEARCH

Find the words from the word bank hidden in the puzzle and circle them.

```
I  S  K  C  D  C  H  O  R  E  S  F  M  N  Q  P  G  V  T  X
S  S  L  S  H  T  T  A  W  C  P  U  L  N  B  I  I  D  X  M
R  X  H  W  D  G  A  Z  X  I  H  A  N  O  P  O  D  K  F  Z
U  X  U  E  M  Y  H  V  P  T  S  R  A  K  W  P  J  N  L  J
N  W  C  S  E  L  P  D  L  G  N  E  U  R  Q  L  A  Z  O  J
J  S  O  B  Y  P  S  Y  T  D  S  I  Z  A  B  F  C  Z  H
I  Y  E  R  L  T  R  I  C  K  C  H  K  C  S  B  O  M  K  W
X  B  B  P  K  K  Q  R  X  W  M  V  F  H  D  N  B  A  G  T
J  S  E  V  E  N  U  V  K  I  R  X  I  E  A  O  N  J  O  X
A  S  R  E  I  R  L  Z  X  F  O  U  P  L  Q  X  F  Q  Q  L
G  A  D  E  U  T  T  S  E  E  F  Y  L  H  G  A  G  K  L  E
G  S  F  F  L  X  U  F  R  H  C  C  Q  K  S  U  M  P  Y  N
E  U  H  F  I  H  A  Q  D  L  E  A  H  V  E  K  J  R  P  N
U  Q  G  G  I  U  F  P  H  W  S  D  D  Y  F  Z  M  Z  V  F
L  B  M  M  D  E  P  E  N  D  A  B  L  E  X  F  R  M  A  W
```

WORD BANK

Jacob	wise	Rachel
work	trick	sheep
wife	chores	seven
flock	Leah	dependable

FORGIVING ESAU

When Esau was younger, his twin brother, Jacob, tricked their father into giving Esau's blessing to himself. Esau was very angry! He held a grudge against Jacob for a long time. Esau even vowed to kill him. Jacob was so afraid, he ran away and did not return.

Many years passed and the brothers never saw or talked with each other. Until one day, Esau received word that his brother Jacob was coming home.

Esau was excited to see his brother again. Jacob, however, was afraid that Esau was still angry with him. Yet, when Esau saw his brother, he ran to him, hugged him, and cried with joy. Esau had forgiven him. Jacob was so relieved that his brother forgave him!

God wants us to be able to forgive others, just like Esau forgave Jacob. Sometimes, that is hard to do. But, with God's help, we can forgive.

BEAR WITH EACH OTHER, AND FORGIVE WHATEVER GRIEVANCES YOU MAY HAVE AGAINST ONE ANOTHER. FORGIVE AS THE LORD FORGAVE YOU. COLOSSIANS 3:13

> HAS ANYONE EVER FORGIVEN YOU FOR SOMETHING YOU DID?

Write about or draw a picture of how it felt to be forgiven.

POWER UP!

Jacob thought Esau was still holding a grudge against him for stealing his father's blessing. Imagine how Jacob felt when Esau met him with open arms! In that moment, Jacob experienced the wonder of forgiveness.

Is there someone in your life that you have been holding a grudge against? Pray that God will help you forgive that person.

✦ On the back of this paper, write or draw something that illustrates the question below:

What would you do or say to a person to let them know that you forgive them?

FORGIVING ESAU

Now, it's your turn to be the hero of the story. Write or draw your own comic strip!

BEAR WITH EACH OTHER, AND FORGIVE WHATEVER GRIEVANCES YOU MAY HAVE AGAINST ONE ANOTHER. FORGIVE AS THE LORD FORGAVE YOU. COLOSSIANS 3:13

GOT ANY GRIEVANCES?

NO! GO FORGIVE

FORGI

VENESS

ACTION!

Before you go to bed tonight, kneel and ask God to forgive you for the ways you sinned today. Everybody sins every day. God will forgive and forget about all of your sins when you bring them to Him.

Now, ask **Him** to help you do the same with others. We are to forgive and forget just as God does with us. Is there someone you need to patch things up with? Ask God to help you forgive like **He** has forgiven you.

FORGIVING ESAU

Carrying a grudge against someone rarely turns out the way we want it to. Find out how Tia learned this lesson in this Skit-Toon about forgiveness.

Cast: *Two girls to play Tia and Liz*

Tia :   I know what you're doing and it won't work.

Liz: *(follows Tia)* How do you know what I'm doing?

Tia: I just saw Rachel. You're going to force us to sit down and be best friends again.

Liz: I wasn't going to force you to do anything. Tell me again why you won't forgive Rachel?

Tia: I refuse to forgive her because I don't want to let her off the hook. If I forgive her, she'll think she got away with it. And I'm not going to let that happen.

Liz: So, you're willing to hold this grudge just so she'll be miserable?

Tia: Yes! I want her to be more miserable than she made me! *(looks around for Rachel)* So, is Rachel coming?

Liz: Actually, no, she's waiting for me outside. We're going to the mall to pick up something for Katie's birthday party.

Tia: *(looks shocked)* She's going to the party? It's like nothing's happened at all!

Liz: I know you said you weren't going to the party if Rachel went, but I'd really hate it if you didn't come. Rachel really wants you to go, too.

Tia: I can't believe it! I've been holding a grudge against her for months now. It's not fair! Doesn't she know the pain and suffering I went through to hold a grudge against her?

Liz: Tia, all grudges do is make *you* miserable. We're supposed to forgive each other—like Jesus forgave us.

Tia: You're right, carrying a grudge is no fun, *(starts smiling and looking happy)* but I know something that will be fun—Katie's party!

Liz: So you'll go? But what about Rachel?

Tia: You're right about that, too. I need to forgive Rachel. Right after I take a nap—carrying this grudge has made me tired!

POWER TUNES (SING TO THE TUNE OF "THE BEAR WENT OVER THE MOUNTAIN")

The Lord wants me to forgive you,
The Lord wants me to forgive you,
The Lord wants me to forgive you,
Because he forgave me.

Because he forgave me,
Because he forgave me,
The Lord wants me to forgive you,
Because he forgave me.

FORGIVING ESAU

Fill in the blanks about Jacob and Esau by combining the letters with the picture clues.

E +  AND J +  WERE BROTHERS.

_____ _____

J +  TRICKED E +  . THAT MADE

_____ _____

E +   . J +

_____ _____

AWAY. MEN + E Y +

_____ _____

PASSED. J +  WAS AFRAID E +

_____ _____

 STILL   . BUT,

_____ _____ _____

E +  HAD 4 +  + N J +  .

_____ _____ _____

HONEST JOSEPH

When Joseph was a teenager, his jealous brothers sold him into slavery. Joseph ended up in Egypt at the Pharaoh's palace. Despite his circumstances, Joseph was a good and honest slave, and the Lord blessed him with success in everything he did. Joseph's master knew that he was honest and trustworthy in all that he did, so he put Joseph in charge of everything he owned.

Unfortunately, the wife of Joseph's master told a lie that got Joseph into a lot of trouble. The lie sent him to jail. But, the Lord was with Joseph. The guards noticed how honest and hardworking Joseph was and rewarded him with responsibilities and jobs to do, even while in prison.

Joseph was never afraid to tell the truth, even when the circumstances and consequences were hard.

God wants us to be honest all of the time, too, no matter what our circumstances are and no matter how hard it may seem.

HAVE YOU EVER BEEN TEMPTED TO LIE TO GET OUT OF TROUBLE?

AN HONEST ANSWER IS LIKE A KISS ON THE LIPS. PROVERBS 24:26

Write about or draw a picture of a time you lied to get out of trouble.

Power Up!

Joseph was honest when times were good, and he was honest when he was a prisoner and things were not-so-good. Telling the truth, no matter what the outcome, is never easy. Being a person with a reputation of honesty makes you someone who can be trusted, just like Joseph was.

God hates all types of dishonesty (Proverbs 12:22). Choose to be honest in all situations. Ask God to help you when tempted to tell a lie.

✦ On the back of this paper, draw something that illustrates the question below:

What can I do if tempted to tell a lie?

HONEST JOSEPH

Now, it's your turn to be the hero of the story. Write or draw your own comic strip!

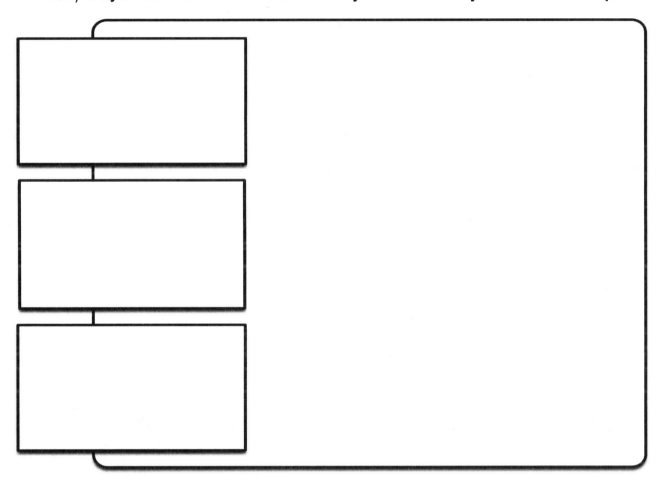

ACTION! Scripture helps us to stand strong against being dishonest. Cut out three small paper flags. On each flag, copy one of these verses from the Bible: Proverbs 24:26, Proverbs 12:22, and Psalm 119:30. Attach the flags to toothpicks and stick them in a small ball of play dough. Keep them in a place to remind you to be honest no matter what the circumstances.

AN HONEST ANSWER IS LIKE A KISS ON THE LIPS.
PROVERBS 24:26

I CANNOT TELL A LIE. I CHOPPED DOWN THE CHERRY—I MEAN—SYCAMORE TREE.

HONEST JOSEPH

God commands us to be honest all the time. Have the students brainstorm specific times that they can be honest. Use the answers to act out a skit, or use the suggestions below.

Child One: I can be honest when I'm playing a game.

Child Two: I can be honest when I'm taking a test.

Child Three: I can be honest when I'm spending money.

Child Four: I can be honest when I'm doing my homework.

Child Five: I can be honest when I'm in trouble.

Child Six: I can be honest when I'm cleaning my room.

Child Seven: I can be honest in the morning.

Child Eight: I can be honest in the afternoon.

Child Nine: I can be honest in the evening.

Everyone: I can be honest all of the time!

POWER TUNES (SING TO THE TUNE OF "LONDON BRIDGE")

Before singing, inflate a balloon. After singing about Joseph, gently tap the balloon in the air to one of the children. The child who catches the balloon taps it in the air over and over as the class sings the next verse, using that child's name. At the end of the verse, the child with the balloon taps it to another child and the singing continues. Sing until each child is recognized.

Joseph was an honest man,
Honest man, honest man.
Joseph was an honest man;
Joseph pleased Jesus.

(Child's name) is an honest (girl/boy),
Honest (girl/boy), honest (girl/boy).
(Child's name) is an honest (girl/boy);
(Child's name) pleases Jesus.

HONEST JOSEPH

Unscramble the words in each sentence to finish the story of Joseph. Then, unscramble the circled letters to find the answer to the bonus question!

1. When _____ _____ _____ _____ _____ ⃝ was a teenager, his brothers sold him.

   (H) (S) (J) (P) (O) (E)

2. Joseph's _____ _____ ⃝ _____ _____ _____ _____ _____ were jealous of him.

   (R) (E) (B) (H) (R) (S) (O) (T)

3. They sold Joseph to be a _____ _____ _____ _____ ⃝.

   (L) (A) (E) (S) (V)

4. Joseph was a slave in Pharaoh's house in _____ _____ _____ _____ ⃝.

   (Y) (G) (T) (P) (E)

5. Joseph's _____ _____ ⃝ _____ _____ _____ saw that the Lord was with him.

   (S) (A) (E) (M) (T) (R)

6. The Lord was with Joseph even when he was in _____ _____ _____ _____ _____ ⃝.

   (O) (R) (P) (S) (I) (N)

BONUS QUESTION!

According to Proverbs 24:26, what kind of answer is like a kiss on the lips?

An _____ _____ _____ _____ _____ _____ one.

TRUSTING MOSES

One day God appeared to Moses in the flames of a burning bush and asked him to do a very big job. God instructed Moses to go to Egypt and free the Israelites from slavery. At first, Moses did not think he could ever do this big job. Who would listen to him? But, God told Moses not to be afraid and that He would be with him every step of the way. Moses trusted God and obeyed whatever He commanded.

There were times when Moses felt afraid and overwhelmed with what God was asking him to do, yet Moses' trust in God was unshakable. With God by his side, Moses finally led the Israelites out of Egypt. Even when the Pharaoh changed his mind and cornered the Israelites against the Red Sea, Moses trusted in God's promise of deliverance. Even when everyone around him was doubting they would ever escape, Moses' trust in God never failed. Moses knew God would save them—provide a way of escape—and that is exactly what He did. God parted the Red Sea allowing only the Israelites to pass through to safety.

. . .IN GOD I TRUST; I WILL NOT BE AFRAID. WHAT CAN MAN DO TO ME? PSALM 56:11

HAVE YOU EVER FELT OVERWHELMED BY A BIG JOB?

Write about or draw a picture of a big job you had to do.

POWER UP!

What did God ask Moses to do? Why didn't Moses want the job at first?

We all get overwhelmed and even scared at times when faced with big tasks or challenges. God wants us to trust Him to help us through it all. He promises to be with us every step of the way. Even in the most difficult situations, when we feel cornered and afraid, place your trust in God. He will open up a way for you and help you through it all.

✦ On the back of this paper, draw or write something that will illustrate the question below:

How can you show God you trust Him, even in the most difficult of times?

Now, it's your turn to be the hero of the story. Write or draw your own comic strip!

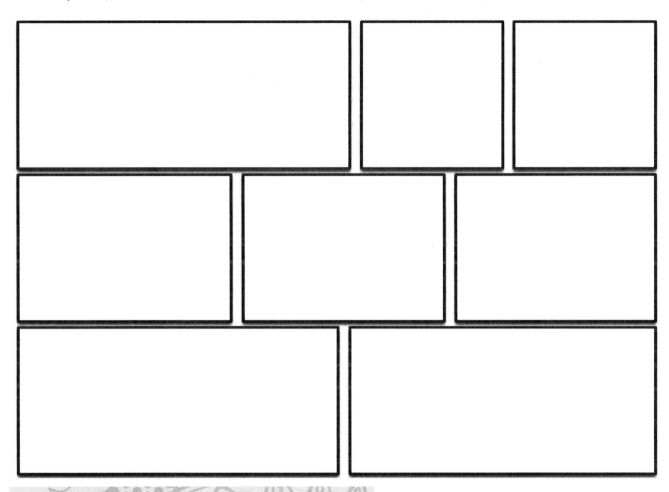

. . . IN GOD I TRUST; I WILL NOT BE AFRAID. . . . PSALM 56:11

I WAS TALKING TO THIS BUSH, IF YOU DON'T MIND.

ACTION! Fold an 8 ½" x 11" piece of white paper vertically so that the left and right ends meet in the middle. Open up the two folded panels and copy the verse, Psalm 56:11, on the middle of the page. Anytime you are feeling afraid, open up your card to reveal the Bible verse. Pray that God will open up a way for you to get through tough times, just like He did with the Israelites.

TRUSTING MOSES

To make the props for this Skit-Toon, have the students draw sea creatures on two sheets of blue bulletin board paper. Place the paper on the floor with long edges touching and the decorated side facing down. In addition, have the students decorate a poster board to look like fire.

Cast: *God (voice), Moses, Aaron, Pharaoh, Israelites (class)*

God: *(Sits and speaks from behind the fire poster board. Moses stands in front of the poster)* Moses, return to Egypt. I need you to set my people free from slavery.

Moses: Oh, not me, God. That job is too big for me!

God: Trust in me. I will be with you. *(Exit scene.)*

Moses: In God I trust; I will not be afraid. *(Walk over to Aaron.)* Aaron, we're going on a trip.

Aaron: A trip? Where are we going?

Moses: God wants us to set his people free from Egypt.

Aaron: God wants us to do what?

Moses: Just trust Him. If He asks us to do a job, you can trust He's going to help us.

Aaron: In God I trust; I will not be afraid. *(Both walk to Israelites.)*

Moses: Hey everybody! God wants us to lead you to the promised land.

Israelites: But, we're afraid!

Moses: Put your trust in God.

Israelites: In God we trust; we will not be afraid.

Pharaoh: Let the Israelites go! These plagues are unbearable! *(Moses and Israelites start walking away towards "sea")*

Pharaoh: What have I done? We need those slaves back! *(Slowly follow the Israelites.)*

Israelites: We're being followed. How will we get across the sea?

Moses: Trust God. He'll show a way!

Israelites: In God we trust, we will not be afraid.

Moses: Follow me. *(Four Israelites hold up paper to leave an opening in the middle. Walk through the opening ("water"). When everyone is on the other side, let water fall back down.)*

All: *(Kneel.)* In God we trust; we will not be afraid.

POWER TUNES (SING TO THE TUNE OF "THE FARMER IN THE DELL")

Verse 1	Verse 2	Verse 3
Moses trusted God.	Moses trusted God.	I can trust in God.
Moses trusted God.	Moses trusted God.	I can trust in God.
He heard him from a burning bush,	He walked right through the deep, deep sea.	I'll trust God like Moses did.
Moses trusted God.	Moses trusted God.	I can trust in God.

Trusting Moses

MOSES' FILL-IN-THE-BLANK STORY

Choose the picture that completes each sentence. Color the correct picture and write the word represented in the picture on the line.

1. One day God appeared to Moses in a _____

2. Moses told the _____ to let his people go.

3. _____ went with Moses to help him free the Hebrew people.

4. One of the plagues God sent was _____.

  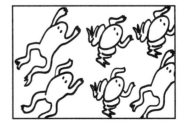

COURAGEOUS JOSHUA

One of the most courageous men in the Bible is Joshua. After Moses died, Joshua became leader of the Israelites. Leading millions of people across a desert was not an easy job. God told Joshua, however, to be strong and courageous for He would be with him wherever he went.

Joshua was courageous in leading God's people across the flooded Jordan River. Joshua followed God's instructions and the water parted and let the Israelites safely cross to the other side. Joshua then told the people to stack 12 stones, taken from the riverbed, as a reminder of God's power.

Joshua was also courageous when conquering the land. In one battle, God told Joshua to march around the city of Jericho once a day for six days. On the seventh day, God said to march around the city seven times and blow trumpets. On the seventh day, the walls of Jericho fell down and the Israelites took the land God had promised them.

Joshua faced many impossible situations, yet he faced each one with courage because he knew that God was with him.

BE STRONG AND COURAGEOUS. DO NOT BE TERRIFIED; DO NOT BE DISCOURAGED, FOR THE LORD YOUR GOD WILL BE WITH YOU WHEREVER YOU GO. JOSHUA 1:9

HAVE YOU EVER FACED AN IMPOSSIBLE SITUATION?

Write about or draw a picture of a time when you faced a situation that seemed impossible.

POWER UP! Joshua courageously faced many impossible situations. He obeyed God no matter what. He always trusted wholeheartedly that God was with him wherever he went. When he led the Israelites across the flooded Jordan river, Joshua told his men to get stones from the river as a reminder of God's power. When something seems impossible, be courageous and look to the impossible things God took care of in the past to know that God can take care of anything—and that He will be with you wherever you go.

✦ On the back of this paper, draw something that illustrates the question below:

How can I be courageous when facing a tough situation?

Now, it's your turn to be the hero of the story. Write or draw your own comic strip!

ACTION! Look for stones or rocks to make your own reminders to be brave when facing the impossible. Wash the rocks to remove any dirt before beginning. Using permanent markers or paint, write *Be Strong*, or *Be Brave*, or any other phrase on the rocks that will remind you to lean on God when things look impossible. Carry the rocks with you in your pocket or display them in a place you can see them every day.

BE STRONG AND COURAGEOUS. DO NOT BE TERRIFIED; DO NOT BE DISCOURAGED. . . . JOSHUA 1:9

JOSHUA'S WRECKING CREW
GUARANTEED
Completed in 7 Days
If you got a wall that needs to fall, all you need is time and a trumpet's call!

COURAGEOUS JOSHUA

SKIT-TOON

Cast: *Tyler (boy), Mom, and Dad.*

Mom: Tyler, have you pulled that loose tooth yet?

Tyler: Not yet, Mom—I'm afraid!

Dad: But, Tyler, your permanent tooth is about to come in.

Tyler: I know, but I'm still afraid!

Mom: Tyler, do you remember what God told Joshua in the Old Testament just before making him the leader of His people?

Tyler: Yes. "Be strong and courageous." But, what does that have to do with my tooth?

Dad: God also told him, "Do not be terrified or discouraged, for the Lord your God will be with you wherever you go."

Tyler: Well . . . I still don't see what that has to do with my tooth.

Mom: You see, Tyler, you don't have to be afraid. God is with you and He can give you the courage to pull your tooth.

Dad: You can do it, Tyler; I know you can. Be strong and courageous.

Tyler: I guess I can try. Hey! I've got it! I'll wiggle my tooth every day for six days, and then on the seventh day, I'll wiggle it really hard until it comes out.

Dad: Now there's an idea!

Mom: You really *do* remember the lesson about Joshua, don't you?

Tyler: Sure do! Now if you'll excuse me, I need to work on my battle of Jericho—um, I mean my tooth!

POWER TUNES (SING TO THE TUNE OF "SKIP TO MY LOU")

Have students sit in a circle on the floor. Choose one person to be Joshua. Have that person stand outside the circle. While singing, Joshua skips around the "Jericho" circle. At the end of the song, Joshua taps a person on the head, that person chases Joshua, and Joshua tries to run all of the way around, back to the empty spot. The new person stands outside the circle and play continues.

Joshua, Joshua, be our leader.
Joshua, Joshua, be our leader.
Joshua, Joshua, be our leader.
Lead us 'cross the Jordan.

God is with me wherever I go
God is with me wherever I go
God is with me wherever I go
He'll be with me always.

COURAGEOUS JOSHUA

Help Joshua find his trumpets! Find and circle 10 hidden trumpets in the picture.

35

DEVOTED DAVID

David, once a shepherd boy, became king of Israel. When David was first anointed king, the Bible says, "the LORD has sought out a man after his own heart and appointed him leader of his people" (1 Samuel 13:14). David loved the Lord. He was devoted to worshipping, praying, and serving God.

HOW MUCH TIME DO YOU SPEND WITH GOD EACH DAY?

David did not always do what was right. Yet, he always turned back to God and asked for forgiveness and changed his ways because his heart was fully devoted to pleasing the Lord.

David did many great things as king. He had his men bring the Ark of the Covenant back to be near the Israelite people. He encouraged the people to worship God, and he planned to build a Temple for God.

David spent much of his time writing songs or psalms in praise of God. Every word of the psalms is an expression of David's devotion and love for the Lord. David's life is an example of true devotion to God. He really was a man after God's own heart.

HOW GREAT YOU ARE, O SOVEREIGN LORD! THERE IS NO ONE LIKE YOU, AND THERE IS NO GOD BUT YOU. . . .

2 SAMUEL 7:22

Write about or draw a picture of what you do to spend time with God.

Power Up!

Name at least three ways David showed his devotion to God.

Being devoted to someone means to give all or a large part of your time to that person. Not only did David do things that pleased God, like building the Temple, he was devoted to spending time with God—learning, praising, and worshipping Him. God wants us to be "after His own heart" as well. He wants us to be devoted to the things that please Him and to spend time with Him in His Word, in prayer, and in worship.

✦ On the back of this paper, draw something that illustrates the question below:

What is one way I am going to devote more time to God today?

DEVOTED DAVID

Now, it's your turn to be the hero of the story. Write or draw your own comic strip!

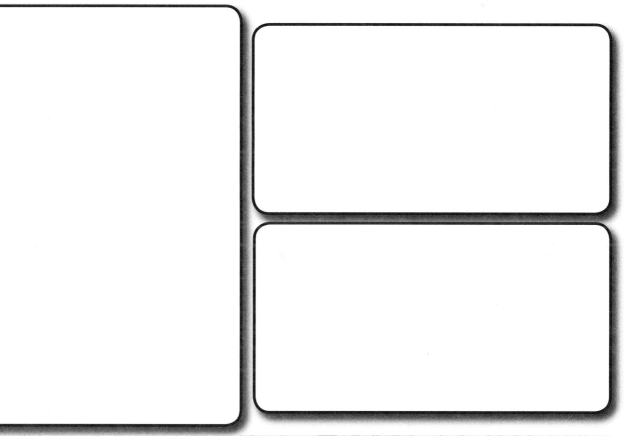

ACTION!

Write your own psalm to God as a way to show your devotion to Him. Read Psalm 8 or Psalm 23 for examples. Write your psalm in a journal, or copy onto a large sheet of construction paper, decorate and hang it where you can see it every day. Be like David and devote time each day to reading—and even writing—psalms.

HOW GREAT YOU ARE, O SOVEREIGN LORD! THERE IS NO ONE LIKE YOU, AND THERE IS NO GOD BUT YOU. . . . 2 SAMUEL 7:22

WHAT DO YOU HAVE THERE?

IT'S MY NEW PSALM PILOT!

DEVOTED DAVID

SKIT-TOON

Before the Skit-toon, make a crown out of construction paper. Then, brainstorm with the class ways that they can show their devotion to God in all that they do. Then, ask the students to write one way they will show their devotion to God on a piece of paper. Have one person wear the crown and say, "I can be devoted to God when I _____." Have the student fill in the blank with what he wrote. Then let the student choose the next person to wear the crown and announce how she will show devotion to God. See examples below.

Child One: I can be devoted to God when I go to church.

Child Two: I can be devoted to God when I do my best in school.

Child Three: I can be devoted to God when I pray.

Child Four: I can be devoted to God when I play soccer.

POWER TUNES (SING TO THE TUNE OF "DO YOU KNOW THE MUFFIN MAN?")

Oh, do you know what David did,
What David did,
What David did,
Oh, do you know what David did,
When he became the king.

King David brought the ark back home
The ark back home,
The ark back home.
King David brought the ark back home,
When he became the king.

King David wrote the book of Psalms
The book of Psalms, the book of Psalms.
King David wrote the book of Psalms,
Because He loved the Lord.

King David loved the Lord, his God
The Lord, his God
The Lord, his God.
King David loved the Lord, his God,
With all his heart and soul.

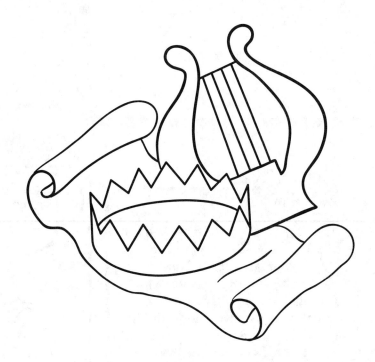

DEVOTED DAVID

Cut out each instrument below and color. Glue each instrument to one of the Israelites in the picture below. Use the blank areas to draw your own musical instruments.

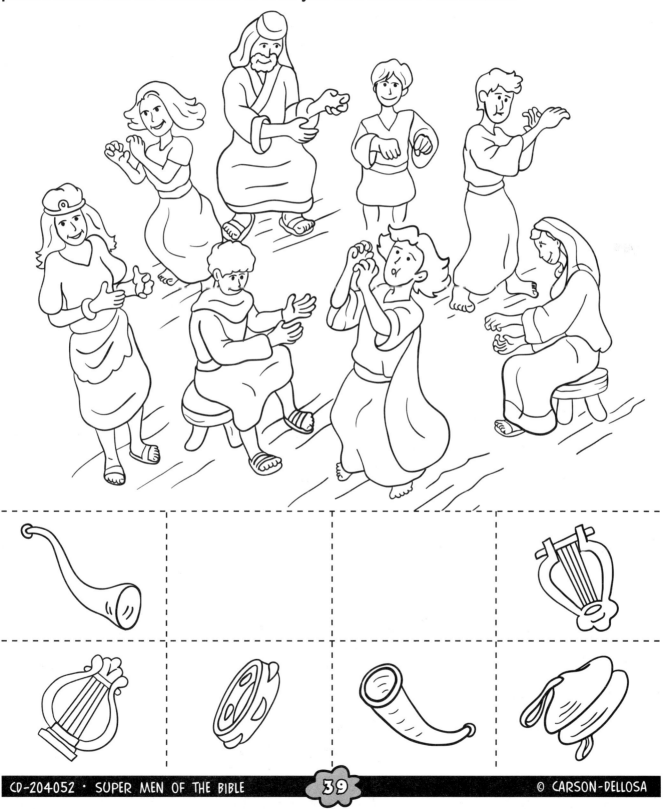

39

PRAYERFUL DANIEL

Daniel was a young man when he was taken captive and sent to Babylon. There, Daniel was surrounded by people who did not know or believe in God. Still, Daniel held strong to his faith and never gave up on his commitment to God— even if it meant his death!

Daniel had a gift of interpreting dreams, which made him one of the king's most trusted advisors. This privileged position made some people angry. They plotted Daniel's death by tricking the king to outlaw prayer to anyone except the king.

In spite of this law, Daniel continued to pray as he always had—three times a day. He knew that God was the only One who could provide the strength he needed during this difficult time. So, Daniel got down on his knees and prayed.

Daniel was thrown into a lion's den for breaking the law against the king. But, God protected Daniel from the lions. Daniel trusted in God and never stopped praying.

DO YOU PRAY REGULARLY?

BE JOYFUL ALWAYS; PRAY CONTINUALLY; GIVE THANKS IN ALL CIRCUMSTANCES. . . .

I THESSALONIANS 5:16–18

Write about or draw a picture of a time when you pray most often.

Power Up!

Why didn't Daniel stop praying to God even when there was a law against it?

Daniel prayed regularly. He didn't just pray when things got rough, or when he needed something. The Bible says that Daniel got down on his knees, giving thanks to God, three times a day. Prayer was Daniel's lifeline to God and he didn't let anything get in the way of his prayer time. We sometimes forget to pray when things are going our way, or when our lives get busy. The Bible tells us to pray continually. Prayer is our lifeline to God.

✦ On the back of this paper, draw something that illustrates the question below:

What do I need to change in my life so I can pray regularly?

PRAYERFUL DANIEL

Now, it's your turn to be the hero of the story. Write or draw your own comic strip!

Action!

Start a list of ways God has been a lifeline to you. Keep this list handy. Every time you think of another reason to be thankful, add it to the list.

During your daily prayer time, use this list to give thanks to God for being your lifeline in good times and in tough times. Make it a habit to add to the list and pray daily!

BE JOYFUL ALWAYS; PRAY CONTINUALLY. . . .
I THESSALONIANS 5:16-17

. . . AND I EVEN PROGRAMMED IT TO PRAY EVERY DAY AT 7:00 A.M. IN CASE I FORGET.

PRAYERFUL DANIEL

SKIT-TOON

Cast: *Sunday school teacher and Adam. Adam should kneel or sit, as if praying.*

Teacher: Adam, what are doing? You should be in Sunday school with the other children.

Adam: I'm praying.

Teacher: Oh, is there anything wrong?

Adam: No, I'm just praying.

Teacher: Well, couldn't you find another time to pray since it is time for Sunday School?

Adam: I usually pray early in the morning.

Teacher: Really? How early?

Adam: I get up around five.

Teacher: Wow, that's early. Why couldn't you pray at night before you go to bed?

Adam: Oh, I do that, too.

Teacher: So, you pray at night and in the morning?

Adam: Yes, but I had to watch my little brother this morning, so that's why I'm praying now. Do you pray?

Teacher: Yes, I pray. Maybe not twice a day. Are you sure there isn't anything wrong?

Adam: No, I told you there's nothing wrong. Just praying to God—like we're supposed to.

Teacher: You're also supposed to be in Sunday School class right now.

Adam: I know. I'll be there in just a minute. I just have one more person to pray for.

Teacher: Do you want me to pray with you?

Adam: Sure. (*Teacher sits down next to Adam. Both close their eyes.*) Dear God, thank You for my Sunday school teacher. She has taught me to pray to you continually and I'm thankful for that. Amen. (*Both open their eyes.*)

Teacher: (*Puts arm around Adam*) Thank you, Adam. You just taught *me* a great lesson today.

POWER TUNES (SING TO THE TUNE OF "WHERE IS THUMBKIN?")

Daniel prayed, Daniel prayed.
Yes he did, Yes he did.
Getting on his knees,
Giving thanks to God,
Daniel prayed, Daniel prayed.

I will pray, I will pray.
Yes I will, Yes I will.
I'll get down on my knees.
Giving thanks to God,
I will pray, I will pray.

DANIEL'S RIDDLE

Unscramble the words by placing one letter on each line. Then, use the numbered letters to complete the answer to the riddle at the bottom of the page.

NED ___ ___ ___

NOISL ___ ___ ___ ___ ___
$\quad\quad$ 5

NGIK ___ ___ ___ ___
$\quad\quad\quad\quad$ 2 $\quad$ 3

UTRTS ___ ___ ___ ___ ___

RYAP ___ ___ ___ ___

HREET ___ ___ ___ ___ ___

NEKSE ___ ___ ___ ___ ___
$\quad\quad\quad\quad\quad\quad$ 4

TICKR ___ ___ ___ ___ ___

IHTFA ___ ___ ___ ___ ___
$\quad\quad$ 1

RIDDLE: Who did God send to help Daniel?

ANSWER: ___ ___ ___ ___ ___ ___ ___
$\quad\quad\quad$ 1 $\quad$ 2 $\quad$ 1 $\quad$ 2 $\quad$ 3 $\quad$ 4 $\quad$ 5

LOVING JOSEPH
FATHER OF JESUS

The Bible describes Joseph as a just and righteous man—meaning he was honest and obeyed the laws of the time. Joseph also loved God with all of his heart.

When Joseph first found out that Mary, the woman he was to marry, was carrying a child, he was afraid. God knew Joseph's heart so He sent an angel who appeared to Joseph in a dream. The angel told Joseph not to be afraid to take Mary as his wife.

God entrusted the Savior of the world to Joseph's faithful and loving care. God knew Joseph would be the most loving, caring father for His Son.

Joseph loved God so much, he obeyed everything He told him to do. He took Mary as his wife, and he became the loving father of God's Son.

Joseph loved Mary and Jesus. God wants us to be loving to our family members, to our friends, neighbors, and even to those people who are difficult to love. It makes God very happy when we love others.

WE LOVE BECAUSE HE FIRST LOVED US. 1 JOHN 4:19

WHO DO YOU LOVE?

Write about or draw a picture of someone you love.

Power Up!

When we show our love to our friends and family, and even to those who are difficult to love, we show people that our faith in God and our relationship with Him is based on love. God tells us to love others so that they will see *His* love. God's love for us is unconditional. That means that he loves us no matter what we do or don't do. That's the kind of love He wants us to show to others.

Thank God for His love and ask Him to help you show His love to others.

✦ On the back of this paper, draw something that illustrates the question below:

What are some ways you can show God's love to others?

Now, it's your turn to be the hero of the story. Write or draw your own comic strip!

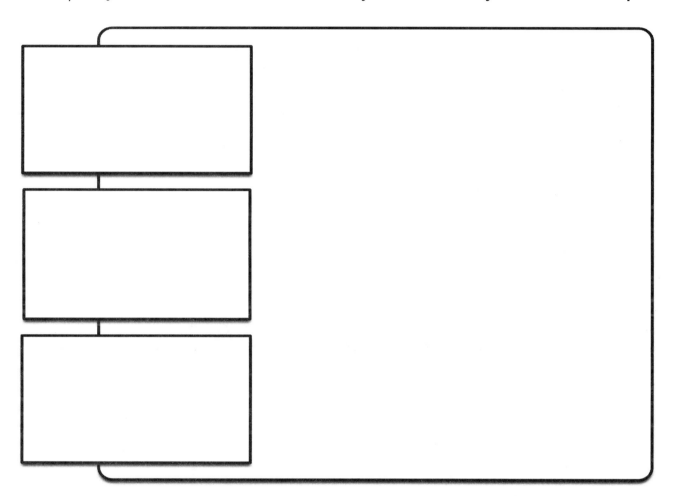

ACTION! God says we should love Him and others. Read 1 Corinthians 13:4–7. These verses explain how we should lovingly treat others. Write on different index cards each thing these verses say about how we should love others. When your whole family is together, like at mealtime, have each person draw one of the cards. Then, have each person tell about a time when someone in the family showed this kind of love.

45

LOVING JOSEPH
FATHER OF JESUS

Cast: Mary, Joseph, angel

Mary: Joseph, we're going to have a baby. God wants us to raise His Son, Jesus.

Joseph: Oh, dear me! Can I really do all that is asked of me?

Mary: God loves us. He wants us to love and raise His Son.

Joseph: I know that God loves us; He loves us very much. (*Walks away from Mary. Lays down to sleep.*)

Angel: Joseph, do not be afraid to take Mary home as your wife, for the child she carries is from the Holy Spirit. She will give birth to a son, and you are to give Him the name Jesus. God loves you, Joseph. And He wants you to love His Son, Jesus.

Joseph: (*Sits up, rubs eyes, looks up towards heaven.*) Thank You for loving me. I do love You, God, and I'll love Your Son, Jesus, too.

POWER TUNES (SING TO THE TUNE OF "HUSH LITTLE BABY")

Sleep, baby Jesus, close your eyes.
Daddy's going to stay right by your side.
Sleep while the stars are up above.
Daddy's going to show you all his love.

Sleep, baby Jesus, close your eyes.
Mommy's going to stay right by your side.
Sleep while the stars are up above.
Mommy's going to show you all her love.

Watch me, Jesus, with your eyes.
I want to be right by your side.
Watch me and love me from above.
I'm going to show You all my love.

Help me, Jesus, to show Your love.
Watch me and love me from above.
Your love for me—let others see.
So they can love You, just like me.

LOVING JOSEPH
FATHER OF JESUS

Joseph was a carpenter who probably taught Jesus how to be a carpenter. Help Joseph find his hidden tools.

HIDDEN PICTURES

hammer   saw   ruler   sawhorse   pencil   wood   nail

DILIGENT
JOHN THE BAPTIZER

God sent a man named John to tell the people that the Messiah was coming. John took this job very seriously, after all, his job was to prepare the way for the Savior of the world!

John lived in the desert and ate locusts and wild honey. He also wore clothes made of camel hair. People came to him from everywhere to hear him preach. John told everyone to repent (turn away from their sins) and be baptized. He was so diligent in his preaching and baptizing that he became known as John the Baptizer. He also reminded people that he baptized with water, but that one day very soon, One would come and baptize with the Holy Spirit. He was talking about Jesus.

Not everyone believed John the Baptizer's message. Yet, he never gave up. John diligently spread the news about the Messiah. He didn't stop until the day Jesus came to him, was baptized, and it was revealed that He was the Promised One who John preached about.

Because of John's diligence, many people were baptized and repented of their sins.

> . . . GO AND MAKE DISCIPLES OF ALL NATIONS, BAPTIZING THEM IN THE NAME OF THE FATHER AND OF THE SON AND OF THE HOLY SPIRIT. MATTHEW 28:19

HAVE YOU EVER RECEIVED SOME REALLY GOOD NEWS?

Write about or draw a picture of a time you received some good news.

Power Up!

Sharing the good news of the gospel with others is what God calls all of us to do. It is the best news to share—and to receive! However, it is easy to get discouraged when others do not listen to the message of God's love. When this happens, don't give up. Be diligent in witnessing to others about the good news of Jesus Christ. Continue to ask God to open up people's hearts to His love and to give you the courage to keep sharing. Only God's love can change people's hearts. Your part is to pray, stick with it, and let Jesus' light shine in your life for everyone to see.

✦ On the back of this paper, draw something that illustrates the question below:

How can you share the good news with someone this week?

Now, it's your turn to be the hero of the story. Write or draw your own comic strip!

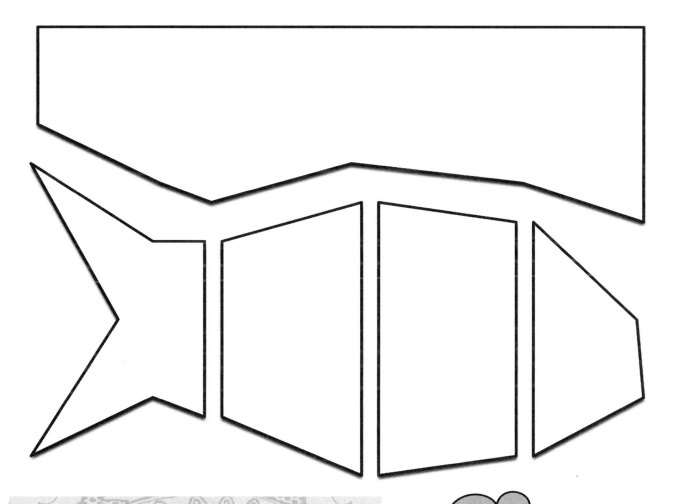

. . . GO AND MAKE DISCIPLES OF ALL NATIONS. . . .
MATTHEW 28:19

SAVES ME TIME WHEN SHARING THE GOSPEL!

ACTION! Use a 3" x 5" index card to help you be diligent in sharing the good news of the gospel. Write three names of non-Christian friends on your card. First, pray 3 x 5—three people, five minutes a day—for God to open up their hearts to Him. Then, ask God for the opportunity and the courage to share the good news of His Son. Be diligent! Keep praying and sharing!

DILIGENT
JOHN THE BAPTIZER

SKIT-TOON

Cast: *John the Baptizer and the entire class, or choose separate children to speak alternating lines.*

John the Baptizer: Hear what I say; Repent and turn away.

All: Tell us one more time; Let us hear your rhyme.

John the Baptizer: Hear what I say; Repent and turn away.
Always do what's right. And pleasing in God's sight.

All: Tell us one more time; Let us hear your rhyme.

John the Baptizer: Always do what's right. And pleasing in God's sight.
Make Jesus "number one." Believe in God's own Son.

All: Tell us one more time; Let us hear your rhyme.

John the Baptizer: Make Jesus "number one." Believe in God's own Son.
Let other people know, that Jesus loves them so.

All: We'll let others know, that Jesus loves them so!

POWER TUNES (SING TO THE TUNE OF "EENSY WEENSY SPIDER.")

John lived in the desert and
Preached to all who'd hear.
"Repent of all your sins
Because the time is near."
The Messiah is coming
To bring us hope and love.
So, turn from sin and prepare your hearts
For God's beloved Son.

I will be so diligent
In spreading the good news
Of the love of Jesus Christ
And the power of the Truth.
I won't give up, no matter what they say
Because Jesus is my Savior
And I'll be with Him one day.

DILIGENT
JOHN THE BAPTIZER

SHAPE CODE SCRAMBLE

Unscramble the words to finish the story of John the Baptizer. Write the letters that are in the polygons and squares in the correct shapes below. Then, unscramble the letters to answer the bonus questions!

1. ___ ___ ___ ___ ___ the ___ ___ ___ ___ ___ ___ ___ ___ ___

N J O H   Z A T P I B E R

told others about ___ ___ ___ ___ ___ .

S S U J E

2. He ___ ___ ___ ___ ___ ___ ___ in the ___ ___ ___ ___ ___ .

D E E P A R C H   D R E E S T

3. He told the ___ ___ ___ ___ ___ to ___ ___ ___ ___ ___ ___ .

E O E P L P   T R E E P N

4. John the Baptizer said, "I ___ ___ ___ ___ ___ ___ with

Z A T P I B E

___ ___ ___ ___ ___ , but Jesus will baptize with the ___ ___ ___ ___ Spirit."

R A W T E   Y O H L

BONUS QUESTION: What did John the Baptizer eat?

⬡ ⬡ ⬡ ⬡ ⬡ ⬡ ▢ ▢ ▢ ▢ ▢

ANSWER: ___ ___ ___ ___ ___ ___ ___ and ___ ___ ___

GENEROUS ZACCHAEUS

Zacchaeus was a dishonest tax collector who lived in the town of Jericho. Zacchaeus was also a very wealthy man because he had cheated many people out of their money.

One day, Jesus came to Jericho. Zacchaeus wanted to see Jesus. Because he was a short man, he could not see over the crowds. So, he ran ahead of the crowd and climbed a sycamore tree to get a better view.

When Jesus came near, He looked up into the tree and said, "Zacchaeus, come on down; I'm going to your house today." Zacchaeus climbed down the tree and welcomed Jesus with open arms.

Zacchaeus knew what he had done was wrong. After meeting Jesus, his heart was changed. Zacchaeus wanted everyone to know his change of heart. He told Jesus that he would give half of his possessions to the poor and return four times the amount of money to all that he cheated. A once greedy and selfish man gave generously to the poor and to all he had hurt over the years.

A GENEROUS MAN WILL PROSPER; HE WHO REFRESHES OTHERS WILL HIMSELF BE REFRESHED. PROVERBS 11:25

HAVE YOU EVER RECEIVED A GIFT THAT WAS MORE THAN YOU EXPECTED?

Write about or draw a picture of a generous gift you've received.

POWER UP!

What did Zacchaeus decide to do after he met Jesus?

Even though Zacchaeus was a greedy man, Jesus loved him. This love changed Zacchaeus on the inside. He wanted others to see his change so Zacchaeus gave generously to the poor and to those he had cheated over the years. The gift of Jesus' forgiveness was more than Zacchaeus ever expected. It made him want to generously share this gift of love with others.

✦ On the back of this paper, draw something that illustrates the question below:

How can I give generously to others?

Now, it's your turn to be the hero of the story. Write or draw your own comic strip!

ACTION!

You can share God's love by giving freely to those in need. Go through your clothes and toys and place the things you no longer use or wear in boxes. Ask someone in your church or community if there is a needy family with a boy or girl who could use what you have outgrown. Perhaps your town has a food pantry to which you could donate some canned goods. Involve your whole family in giving to others.

A GENEROUS MAN WILL PROSPER; HE WHO REFRESHES OTHERS WILL HIMSELF BE REFRESHED. PROVERBS 11:25

I CAN'T WAIT TO TELL MY MOTHER THAT MONEY DOES GROW ON TREES.

Generous Zacchaeus

Cast: Zacchaeus, Jesus, and several children.

Children should stand in front of a kneeling "Zacchaeus." Have a chair nearby for a pretend "tree." Then, Jesus enters, walking slowly past the people.

Child One: Look! It's Jesus!

Zacchaeus: I can't see anything!

Child Two: Jesus is here!

Zacchaeus: I can't see anything!

Child Three: Jesus is coming this way!

Zacchaeus: I can't see anything! (*Climbs onto the chair; peeks over the crowd.*)

Jesus: (*Stops in front of the crowd; look up at Zacchaeus.*) My friend, Zach. Come down from the tree. I'm going to your house today.

Zacchaeus: But I am a sinner!

Jesus: Turn from your sins. Take care of the ones you have cheated.

Zacchaeus: I will never cheat again. I'll help those in need. I will give them back their money, plus extra money!

POWER TUNES (SING TO THE TUNE OF "FARMER IN THE DELL")

Zacchaeus was so small.
He couldn't see the Lord.
He climbed up in a sycamore,
And there was his reward.

Jesus looked in the tree.
"Friend, now come on down.
I'm going to your house tonight.
Once lost, but now you're found."

Zacchaeus, he did say,
"I'll give my wealth away.
I'll sin no more, I'll do what's right,
For I've been saved today!"

A TREE FOR ZACCHAEUS

Fill in the missing words to Proverbs 11:25 using the words from the Word Bank. One word will be used twice.

_____ _____ _____

m _____ _____ _____ _____ _____

_____ _____ _____ _____ _____ _____ ;

h e _____ _____ _____ _____

_____ _____ _____ _____ _____ _____ s

_____ _____ _____ _____ _____ i

m _____ _____ _____ _____ _____

_____ _____ _____ _____ .

WORD BANK

refreshed	refreshes
man	others
will	generous
A	prosper
who	be
himself	

PREPARED PHILIP

Philip was one of the seven men chosen by the apostles to help distribute food among the poor. He was also one of the first traveling missionaries who spread the good news of salvation to all people. Philip was a wise student of the Bible. He could explain its meaning clearly and was always prepared to share the gospel.

Philip was in Samaria preaching when an angel of the Lord told him to go to a desert road. Philip obeyed and went where God sent him. While on this road, Philip saw an Ethiopian official riding in a chariot and reading from the book of Isaiah. Philip asked the Ethiopian official if he understood what he was reading. The man replied that he did not understand and invited Philip into his chariot to explain. Philip was ready. He explained how Jesus was the fulfillment of the prophecies found in the book of Isaiah and shared the good news of Jesus.

Because Philip obeyed God and was prepared to share about Jesus, the Ethiopian man was baptized.

ALWAYS BE PREPARED TO GIVE AN ANSWER TO EVERYONE WHO ASKS YOU TO GIVE THE REASON FOR THE HOPE THAT YOU HAVE.
I PETER 3:15

HAVE YOU EVER BEEN UNPREPARED?

Write about or draw a picture of a time when you were unprepared for a test.

POWER UP!

You never know when God is going to call you to share your faith—it is sort of like a pop quiz. How prepared are you? Write a paragraph or two about who Jesus is, and how He has changed your life. Write it as if you are sharing this with someone who has never heard of Jesus. Practice reading it aloud, or keep it in your Bible to use next time someone asks you to share your faith.

✦ On the back of this paper, draw something that illustrates the question below:

How can I be prepared to share my faith?

Now, it's your turn to be the hero of the story. Write or draw your own comic strip!

ACTION!

Make Witness Cards as a way to be prepared to share your faith at any time. Cut a piece of card stock into rectangles. On each rectangle, write a Bible verse to share with someone who asks about your faith. Some examples may be: John 3:16, Romans 2:8, Romans 8:38–39 and Romans 10:9. Make as many copies of these verses as you desire. Paper clip them together and tuck them in a place where you can reach them easily. You will always be prepared to share God's Word!

ALWAYS BE PREPARED TO GIVE AN ANSWER TO EVERYONE WHO ASKS YOU TO GIVE THE REASON FOR THE HOPE THAT YOU HAVE. I PETER 3:15

I WANTED TO BE PREPARED WITH ANSWERS IN CASE ANYONE ASKS ME ABOUT JESUS.

PREPARED PHILIP

Cast: *Adam, Daniel, and Will.*

Will should be sitting off to the side reading a Bible.

Adam: Wow, this is a great church camp isn't it?

Daniel: Yeah, I was supposed to go to a friend's birthday party this weekend, but something told me to come here instead.

Adam: Well, I'm going to go to the mess hall for some dinner, are you coming?

Daniel: No, I think I will take a walk down by the lake. I'll get dinner later. *(Adam walks away and Daniel pretends to be taking a walk when he spots Will sitting and reading the Bible. He stops, unsure what to do, then calls out)* Hi. I don't mean to bother you, I was just taking a walk.

Will: *(looks up from reading)* You aren't bothering me. I just needed a quiet place to read.

Daniel: What are you reading?

Will: I'm reading the book of Isaiah.

Daniel: Do you need help understanding it?

Will: Do I ever! I'm new at this, and I'm having a hard time making sense of everything.

Daniel: *(sits next to Will)* Isaiah is one of the prophets sent to tell of the coming of the Messiah—which is Jesus.

Will: So when Isaiah talks about "the lamb," he is talking about Jesus?

Daniel: Yes! Isaiah said that Jesus was the lamb who would be lead to slaughter. See, Jesus died on the cross for our sins. He did this because He loves us so much. He became the sacrifice for all of us.

Will: Tell me more. *(Daniel and Will pretend to read the Bible for a few moments then pretend to pray.)*

Will: Thank you for taking the time to explain things to me, Daniel. You came at just the right time. I am so happy that Jesus is now my Lord and Savior!

POWER TUNES (SING TO THE TUNE OF "ARE YOU SLEEPING?")

Be prepared,
Be prepared,
To spread the News,
Spread the News.
With anyone who needs it,
With anyone who asks you,
Share God's love,
Share God's love.

PREPARED PHILIP

Fill in the blanks for the story about Philip and the Ethiopian man by finding words that rhyme with the picture clues.

Philip met an Ethiopian _____ while traveling down a

rhymes with

a desert _____. The man was reading from God's

rhymes with

_____ when Philip came to his _____.

rhymes with   rhymes with

Philip said, "Let me tell you about Jesus' _____. He gave

rhymes with

His life just for _____. The man said, "Baptize _____."

rhymes with   rhymes with

The Ethiopian man rejoiced and went on his _____.

rhymes with

BOLD PAUL

Before Paul became a believer in Jesus, he hated all Christians. However, after a personal encounter with Jesus on a road to the city of Damascus, Paul became a fearless champion of the Christian church.

Paul had to be bold in preaching the gospel. The Christians were terrified of him, and the Jewish people were astonished and baffled at his new faith. However, the Bible says that Paul grew more and more powerful by proving that Jesus was the Messiah.

Despite the constant danger that surrounded early Christians, Paul boldly preached the Gospel to anyone who would listen. He also wrote letters to various churches. These letters became part of the New Testament.

Paul had so much confidence that Jesus was the Messiah, that he courageously endured prison, beatings, and even a poisonous snake bite for his faith.

The lives Paul touched were blessed and changed by his boldness when telling the good news about Jesus Christ.

HAVE YOU EVER DONE OR SAID SOMETHING THAT WAS BOLD?

NOW, LORD . . . ENABLE YOUR SERVANTS TO SPEAK YOUR WORD WITH GREAT BOLDNESS.
ACTS 4:29

Write about or draw a picture of a time you were bold.

POWER UP!

Being bold means having the confidence and courage to press on through our fears and do what we know is right. When we are confident in God's love, we can live and speak His Word with great boldness! We may not have to face the same dangers Paul faced as a Christian, yet, there may be times you will face rejection for your beliefs. Pray for courage that you, too, can be a fearless champion of the gospel, and that through your boldness, others will be blessed and changed as well.

✦ On the back of this paper, draw something that illustrates the question below:

What is one way I can be bold in my faith?

BOLD PAUL

Now, it's your turn to be the hero of the story. Write or draw your own comic strip!

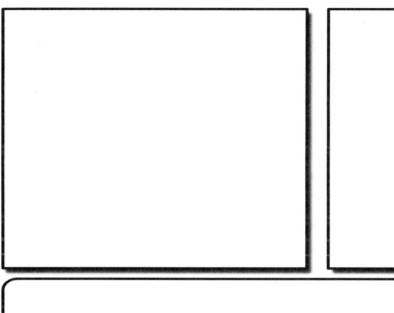

NOW, LORD . . . ENABLE YOUR SERVANTS TO SPEAK YOUR WORD WITH GREAT BOLDNESS. ACTS 4:29

WHY DOES PAUL SPEND SO MUCH TIME IN PRISON?

MAYBE IT'S HIS "ARRESTING" PERSONALITY!

ACTION!

Have you ever received an awesome gift that you could not wait to tell your friends about? That is the kind of excitement you should have about sharing the gift of God's love with others. And remember, you are not alone! You have the Holy Spirit with you to give you the power and confidence to be bold. Ask God to help you be bold about your faith so that you can share it with others. Share the same great gift you have been given!

BOLD PAUL

Cast: *Narrator, Citizen, Guard, Prisoner, Paul, Silas*

Narrator: Paul and his fellow believer, Silas, were spreading the news of Jesus Christ in a town called Phillipi when they got in trouble.

Citizen: I'm tired of your preaching and causing a ruckus around here. Guard, arrest them!

Narrator: Paul and Silas were taken before the king where the people of the town accused them of things they did not even do. The king didn't listen to Paul and Silas and threw them both jail.

(Paul and Silas sit near the other prisoner as the guard watches over them.)

Guard: I'm supposed to watch you closely, so don't try any funny stuff, ok?

Silas: Well, Paul, we're not getting out anytime soon.

Paul: Probably not.

Narrator: So, all night long, they sang hymns to God and prayed.

Prisoner: How can you sing at a time like this? Aren't you afraid?

Paul: I have nothing to be afraid of.

Silas: Hey, who's shaking the jail?

Narrator: It felt like an earthquake was shaking the prison. It went dark and all the jail cell doors fell open and the prisoners ran away (*prisoner runs out of jail*). When it stopped, the guard looked around at the shambles of the jail!

Guard: I'm dead! The king is never going to believe that I lost his prisoners—especially those two apostles!

Paul: Hey, we're still here, don't worry!

Guard: But the jail is open, you could have run for your life!

Silas: We know. Believe me, we know.

Guard: Who are you people?

Paul: We are followers of Jesus Christ. We have been saved by Him.

Guard: How can I be saved?

Narrator: So Paul and Silas told the guard all about Jesus and the good news of salvation.

POWER TUNES (SING TO THE TUNE OF "TWINKLE, TWINKLE")

Verse 1

Paul was brave and Paul was bold.
He told young and he told old
How Jesus came to free and save.
On the cross His life He gave.
Paul was bold about God's Son.
Said he came for everyone.

Verse 2

I'll be brave and I'll be bold.
I'll tell young and I'll tell old,
How Jesus came to free and save.
On the cross His life He gave.
I'll be bold about God's Son.
Sharing His love with everyone.

BOLD PAUL

"CROSS" WORD PUZZLE

Change one letter of each word in the square to make a new word. The first one has been done for you.

T A L L
T [O] L L
T O L [D]
B O L D

S A I D   G R O W L   L O N G

P A U L   C R O S S   S I N S

R E I N

J A I L

L O S T

L I V E

SPEECH BALLOON TEMPLATE

Copy and cut out the speech balloon shapes to use for the My Story section.
Copy and cut out the extra comic strip panel to use as needed.